THE GREAT ARTISTS
& THEIR WORLD
CÉZANNE

NEW
FOREST
PRESS

Publisher: Melissa Fairley
Editor: Guy Croton
Designer: Carol Davis
Production Controller: Ed Green
Production Manager: Suzy Kelly

ISBN: 978-1-84898-315-1
Library of Congress Control Number: 2010925202
Tracking number: nfp0004

Printed in the USA
9 8 7 6 5 4 3 2 1

CONTENTS

INTRODUCTION

Withdrawn, moody, argumentative, and temperamental, Paul Cézanne was shunned and ridiculed throughout his career. His way of painting was just too different for many of his contemporaries to understand, yet within a year of his death, his work was exhibited in Paris and most of the visitors realized his greatness. His work influenced the direction that art began moving in, making Cézanne one of the most influential artists of the 20th century.

THE FATHER OF MODERN ART

Cézanne's investigation into the underlying structure of everything he painted was a completely new way of representing the world. His ideas had a profound effect on artists such as Gauguin, Matisse, Klee, Picasso, Braque, Gris, Kandinsky, and Modigliani. They—and many others—each developed their own methods inspired by his creativity and innovations. Picasso called him "my one and only master…the father of us all," Klee described him as "the supreme master" and Matisse said he was "a kind of benevolent god of painting." Picasso and Braque developed Cubism in recognition of Cézanne's methods of painting objects from several viewpoints at once and other artists built on aspects of his paint application, use of color, and interpretation of the world. It is believed that his work was one of the key factors in moving art towards abstraction.

THE MASTERPIECE

Although we now recognize that Cézanne was a visionary ahead of his time and a major pioneer in the development of modern art, for much of his life, most people thought he was simply eccentric and misguided. In 1885, his best friend Émile Zola wrote a novel called *The Masterpiece* and without telling him before it was published, based the pitiable and unsuccessful main character on Cézanne. It was obvious from the character's appearance, life, and attitude who it described and naturally, it hurt Cézanne deeply. The two men were never friends again.

But Zola had recognized his genius earlier on and several of the avant-garde artists of the time were aware of his outstanding ability and significance. So nothing was ever straightforward with Cézanne. Reactions to him and his personality were always a mixture of contradictions. He knew what he was aiming for and spent his entire life working on his artistic ideas. He was confident that he was working toward an important development in art, but he was also often unsure and anxious that he was not doing it thoroughly or well enough. He took painstaking care with every painting, but often despaired when he had finished because he did not believe it was good enough or that he would ever achieve his goals. He was the first artist to completely break with the traditions of western painting that dated back to the fifteenth century and he spent his life painting against conventions, despite the hostility of many— including art officials, art teachers, other artists, critics, complete strangers, friends, and his family.

INDEPENDENCE

With a childhood dominated by his father, a wealthy banker, Cézanne moved to Paris to study art when he was twenty-one. At that time, the future Impressionists were developing new ideas in art that shook the official French art world. Cézanne mixed with many of them and although he exhibited with them twice and was interested in their independent ideas, his own goals were always different from theirs. Even more radical than they were, he aimed to capture both what we see and what we do not see—the underlying structures of things – and his colorful, patchy paintings focused less on realism than on elements such as structure, harmony, color, and brushstrokes. While the Impressionists were trying to make their new ideas noticed and accepted in Paris, Cézanne spent most of his time painting in his quiet family home in Aix-en-Provence, feeling uncomfortable in the sophisticated capital of France where he was frequently mocked by critics. He spent hours studying his subjects before he even made a mark, he worked out precisely where everything would be on the canvas and agonized over every brushstroke before applying them. He worked mainly in solitude as he never seemed to fit in with any one particular group and he said that his ambition was to "make of Impressionism something solid and durable like the art of museums."

THE WORLD OF CÉZANNE

Paul Cézanne was born on the January 19, 1839, in Aix-en-Provence in the south of France. Paul was the eldest of three children born to Louis-Auguste Cézanne and Anne-Élisabeth Aubert. Paul's father made enough money as a felt-hat trader to become a banker, founding the Cézanne and Cabassol Bank in Aix in 1848. Paul grew up in a secure, well-to-do family home with his two sisters enjoying the pleasant climate and attractive countryside surrounding Aix. When he was 13 years old he attended the Collège Bourbon in Aix as a boarder, and it was here he met Émile Zola who was to become a lifelong friend. Cézanne and Zola, together with a third friend Jean Baptiste Baille, became known to their school friends as the "Inseparables" who enjoyed nothing more than long walks in the countryside, fishing, and swimming in the nearby river Arc. Cézanne, encouraged by his father to study Law, eventually enrolled at the university of Aix.

AIX-EN-PROVENCE, c.1900

Approximately 20 miles (32 km) north of the Mediterranean port of Marseilles and 400 miles (650 km) south of Paris, Aix-en-Provence was a provincial town which proved idyllic for the growing child, but a conservative backwater for the young intellectual. Émile Zola left for Paris as soon as he had finished at the Collège Bourbon in 1858, while Cézanne stayed on to enroll at the university and attend life-drawing classes at the local free drawing school. Cézanne's father had decided that legal training was the best course for his son and of most help to the prosperous Cézanne Bank. It was obvious to the young Cézanne, however, that a career as a lawyer was not what he wanted, and he dreamed of joining his friend Zola in Paris and becoming an artist.

PAUL CÉZANNE

It was quite clear that Cézanne was not going to settle down at university in Aix to study Law, nor was he going to follow his father's footsteps into the family bank. Encouraged by Émile Zola, Cézanne decided to head for Paris and try his hand as an artist. Eventually Cézanne's father gave him his blessing and Cézanne traveled to Paris in 1861 to spend the summer with Zola. This was an unhappy time. Cézanne felt an outsider and did not feel comfortable with the sophisticated ways of the city dwellers. He missed the countryside of Provence and after his application to join the École des Beaux-Arts in Paris was turned down he returned, dejected, to Aix. It would not be long however before the urge returned and he made plans to return to Paris with the financial support of his father.

ONE OF FOUR MURALS FROM THE SALON OF THE JAS DE BOUFFAN, 1859

The Jas de Bouffan was generally in a poor state of repair when the Cézanne family moved there, and Paul was given permission to paint on the walls of one of the rooms. In 1859, Cézanne painted a series of murals of the four seasons. These paintings are the earliest known works of Cézanne. The elongated female figures depicted in the murals show Cézanne's knowledge of art of previous generations. They show the distinct influence of artists such as the 16th-century Italian, Sandro Botticelli, and Cézanne himself recognizes his debt by signing the paintings, not in his own name, but that of Ingres, who was famed for his academic style.

HOUSE AND FARM AT THE JAS DE BOUFFAN (DETAIL), 1885/7

In 1859, Louis-Auguste Cézanne purchased a fine 18th-century house with surrounding grounds situated close to the center of Aix. The house had formerly belonged to the Governor of Provence and was called the *Jas de Bouffan* (House of the Wind).

THE ARTIST & HIS TIMES

INFLUENCES & EARLY WORKS

In 1862 Cézanne settled in Paris. Like all aspiring artists he was a frequent visitor to the Louvre, where he spent hours sitting in front of paintings meticulously copying the great masters. This was the established way of learning how to paint and Cézanne was no exception. Gradually he discovered the works of living artists such as Eugène Delacroix, who was a great source of inspiration for artists of Cézanne's generation. Delacroix symbolized rebellion against the Classical art, which dominated the art schools at the time, led by the great French artist and master draughtsman, Jean Auguste Dominique Ingres. The Romantic artists, led by Delacroix, considered color to be more important than draughtsmanship and favored exotic subject matter over the traditional subjects depicted by the followers of Ingres. The École des Beaux-Arts, taught in the Classical tradition, was still favored by the critics and by the public, but it was increasingly out of touch with the new generation of artists. The up-and-coming painters no longer sought the advice and approval of the established system of teaching and they were becoming dissatisfied with the official annual exhibition of paintings at the Salon.

THE STRANGLED WOMAN
(detail), c.1870/2

In his early works painted during the 1860s, Cézanne's rapid fusion of brushstrokes and color borrow from the work of Delacroix, but also appear similar to the pictures of Honoré Daumier, an artist whose cartoons were full of biting political satire. The dark earthy realism of his solid figures could equally owe a debt to Gustave Courbet, whose work would have been known to the young Cézanne. Cézanne experimented with different painterly styles during this period just as he chose to depict a wide range of subject matter, from imaginary scenes of violence to still life.

APOTHEOSIS OF DELACROIX, *c.1870/2*

Cézanne made his palette of colors deliberately bright in emulation of Delacroix. Of color he said: *"Pure drawing is an abstraction. Line and modeling do not count; drawing and outline are not distinct, since everything in nature has color... by the very fact of painting one draws. The accuracy of tone gives simultaneously the light and shape of the object, and the more harmonious the color, the more the drawing becomes precise."*

THE DEATH OF SARDANAPALUS *Eugène Delacroix*

When Delacroix painted this picture in 1829, he was angrily attacked by the art establishment for his use of brilliant color, exotic, and dramatic subject matter, and free handling of the paint, which was seen to be "anti-French" in its rejection of French Classicism. In 1832, he visited north Africa and this opened up a whole new field of subject matter as well as heightening his appreciation of color. He also used literary sources of inspiration including Byron, Scott, and Shakespeare, and his way of painting broke new ground enabling the Realist artists to follow.

Cézanne made a number of copies of Delacroix's paintings as well as making his own pictures which also contained images of violence, such as *The Abduction, The Murder, The Woman Strangled,* and *The Autopsy.*

9

THE HOUSE OF
DR GACHET AT AUVERS, *c.*1873

Cézanne was encouraged by Pissarro to move to a small village near Pontoise called Auvers-sur-Oise. Cézanne stayed with the eccentric art enthusiast Dr Gachet who was a great supporter of the young artists. Pissarro and Cézanne painted landscapes in the pretty countryside.

INFLUENCES &
EARLY WORKS

In Paris, Cézanne mixed with the most modern, adventurous painters and intellectuals who discussed their ideas about art and literature in the Paris cafés, particularly the Café Guerbois in the Batignolles district of Paris. The painter Camille Pissarro became a good friend and introduced Cézanne to artists such as Manet, Monet, and Renoir. Cézanne however did not feel at ease in this company, and complained in a letter *"I am just wasting my time in every respect... just don't go imagining that I shall become a Parisian..."* In 1863 the "Salon des Refusés" was set up to give the public the opportunity to see the works of artists rejected from the official Salon. The picture that caused the greatest sensation at the Salon des Refusés was, *Le Déjeuner sur l'Herbe* by Édouard Manet. The works of Manet and Courbet attempted to be true to life, depicting ordinary scenes of everyday life, *"bringing art into contact with the common people."* Cézanne submitted a number of paintings to the Salon, all of which were rejected.

THE CUTTING, 1870

Cézanne traveled between Paris and his family home in Aix. In 1869 he met his future wife, Hortense Fiquet, who modeled for him when he was working in Paris, and they began living together. In 1870 they moved to the fishing village of L'Estaque, near Marseilles, to avoid the Franco-Prussian war. Cézanne became obsessed with painting the rocky Mediterranean landscape. Around this time he painted the landscape of a railway cutting near Aix. In the distance, behind the cutting, towers the Mont Sainte-Victoire—this feature of the Aix countryside was to dominate Cézanne's painting for the rest of his life.

THE HOUSE OF THE HANGED MAN

This painting was made in 1873, when Cézanne was heavily influenced by the Impressionist style. The painting reveals Cézanne's continuing obsession with representing solidity of form. Heavy brushstrokes give it a physicality anchoring the imagery in the landscape, rather than relying on color to depict light, as in the works of the Impressionist painters. *The House of the Hanged Man* was exhibited at the first Impressionist exhibition where it was purchased by Count Armand Doria for the sum of 300 francs.

PHOTO OF PISSARRO & CÉZANNE

Camille Pissarro (left) had been friends with Cézanne since they first met in Paris at the Académie Suisse in 1861.
Pissarro, who was 10 years older than Cézanne, persuaded him to try painting outdoors. This *en plein air* way of painting was favored by Pissarro and became the hallmark of the Impressionist painters. They believed it was essential to get close to their subjects, to capture what they saw with immediacy. They concerned themselves with the fleeting effects of light on the subject, and rejected the studio-bound method of painting. Pissarro had a profound influence on Cézanne's painting in the early 1870s and was equally influential on other painters of the day. Pissarro was the only artist to exhibit in all eight Impressionist exhibitions.

THE LIFE OF CÉZANNE

~1839~
Paul Cézanne born on January 19 in Aix-en-Provence, eldest of three children

~1844~
Paul's parents, Louis-Auguste Cézanne and Anne-Élisabeth Aubert are married

~1852~
Attends the Collège Bourbon where he meets Émile Zola and Jean Baptiste Baille. The three become best friends

~1857~
Attends the drawing school in Aix

~1859~
Attends the University of Aix to study law

~1861~
Spends the summer in Paris studying art at the Académie Suisse where he meets Pissarro

Reluctantly returns to Aix to work in the family bank

~1862~
Cézanne gives up work and his legal studies to return to Paris with a modest allowance from his father

~1863~
Attends the Académie Suisse once more and meets Impressionist painters Sisley, Monet, and Renoir

~1866~
Submits work to the Paris Salon but is rejected

THE FLOOR STRIPPERS *Gustave Caillebotte*

La Deuxième Exposition (The Second Exhibition) of Impressionism, was held at the art dealer Durand-Ruel's gallery at 11 rue le Peletier in Paris from April 11 to May 9, 1876. One of the paintings that caused a great sensation was *The Floor Strippers* by Gustave Caillebotte. Caillebotte was an extremely talented and wealthy artist. He extended his interest in painting not only by buying artwork, but by exhibiting it alongside his own. This painting depicts workmen stripping the floor of his new Paris apartment.

FOUR GIRLS ON A BRIDGE

Edvard Munch

Artists from all over the world flocked to Paris in the 1870s and 1880s, as its reputation as a vibrant exciting city with the most modern trends in art spread. Wealthy Americans traveled to Paris, some to collect this new art, some to become artists themselves. A young Norwegian painter named Edvard Munch traveled to Paris and much of his formative youth was spent in the city. By 1892 Munch had attracted enough interest to be able to hold a large exhibition of his work in Berlin. His art was very influential and he soon became a powerful factor in the growth of the Expressionist movement. Munch had himself been influenced in Paris by the deeply personal vision expressed in the works of Gauguin and van Gogh.

THE ART OF HIS DAY

Early in his career Cézanne exhibited alongside artists such as Manet, Whistler, and Pissarro. In 1877, Cézanne showed 16 paintings at the third Impressionist exhibition, which was received with a torrent of criticism. Unlike many of his contemporaries Cézanne spent a great deal of time away from Paris, often in his home town of Aix and the nearby Mediterranean village of L'Estaque. Meanwhile fellow Paris-based artists such as Monet, Degas, and Manet continued to defy the critics with their determination to pursue the new style of painting and sweep away the traditional values of art. Manet's paintings of naked women depicted in recognizable settings shocked a public who were used to art which placed them in the socially acceptable realm of classical mythology. Degas' abrupt framing of everyday scenes copied the photographic "snapshot" which was challenging art as a visual record. Monet's *Impression* of a sunrise over water with bold daubs of orange paint was ridiculed by critics whose description of the painting christened the Impressionist movement. Cézanne became increasingly influential himself as he developed his own style alongside the Post-Impressionist artists such as van Gogh, Gauguin, and Seurat.

LITTLE DANCER OF FOURTEEN YEARS

Edgar Degas

This sculpture, originally modeled in wax, incorporates real artifacts such as hair, dancing shoes, gauze tutu, and silk bodice. It was modeled on Marie van Goethem, a dancer at the Paris Opera, who was known to spend much of her time at the local Brasserie de Martyrs, also favored by artists. The incorporation of real materials in the sculpture was considered very shocking at the time. It was finally exhibited, in a glass case, at the sixth Impressionist exhibition.

THE ARTIST'S SON (detail), 1883/5

On January 4, 1872 in Paris, Hortense Fiquet gave birth to a boy who was registered as Paul Cézanne. The artist was an indulgent father who was very attached to his young son. As Paul grew up, Cézanne began to depend upon him to help organize his affairs. He was later to become Cézanne's advisor, taking care of money matters and the sale of his pictures.

THE ARTIST'S FATHER
(detail), 1866

THE LIFE OF CÉZANNE

~1869~
Meets Hortense Fiquet, who models for him, and becomes his mistress

Hortense moves in with Cézanne

~1872~
Son Paul is born

Cézanne, Hortense, and Paul move to the village of Auvers-sur-Oise where Cézanne works with Pissarro

~1874~
Exhibits with the first group exhibition of Impressionist painters

~1877~
Exhibits 16 paintings at the third Impressionist exhibition

~1878~
Cézanne's father threatens to cut off the artist's allowance after hearing of his son's mistress and child who Cézanne had kept a secret

In 1874, already two years after the birth of his son, Cézanne wrote to his parents: *"You ask me why I am not yet returning to Aix. I have already told you in that respect that it is more agreeable for me than you can possibly think to be with you, but that once at Aix I am no longer free and when I want to return to Paris this always means a struggle for me; and although your opposition to my return is not absolute, I am very much troubled by the resistance I feel on your part. I greatly desire that my liberty of action should not be impeded and I shall then have all the more pleasure in hastening my return. I ask Papa to give me 200 francs a month; that will permit me to make a long stay in Aix... believe me, I really do beg Papa to grant me this request and then I shall, I think, be able to continue the studies I wish to make."*

FAMILY, FRIENDS & OTHERS
THE SECRET FAMILY

Cézanne relied heavily on his wealthy parents for financial support. When he moved in with his lover Hortense Fiquet he kept the relationship a secret for fear that his father would cut off his monthly allowance. Cézanne continued to rely upon the financial and emotional support of his family for many years and evidently found it difficult to break free. He secretly established his family in l'Estaque, not far from his parents home in Aix, and continued to spend time with his parents as well as with Hortense, all the time fearful that he would be discovered. Cézanne was also close to his two sisters who shared the promise of the family wealth with him after his father retired from the banking business. The secret of Hortense, and even the birth of Cézanne's son Paul, was kept from his parents but eventually they found out some eight years after Cézanne first met Hortense. Cézanne's father threatened to cut off his son's allowance, forcing Cézanne to seek support from his friends.

MADAME CÉZANNE
IN A RED DRESS, *c.*1890

Cézanne met the 19-year-old Hortense Fiquet in Paris in 1869. Hortense was a young model described as "a tall and handsome brunette with large black eyes." Cézanne, some 11 years her senior, fell in love with her and persuaded her to move in with him. They were not married until 1886, when Cézanne was 47 and his son Paul, 14. Although they stayed together for many years, eventually Cézanne became indifferent to her. After his father's death Cézanne continued to live with his mother and sister Marie in Aix, while Hortense spent most of her time in Paris with their son Paul. One scornful comment gives a good picture of Cézanne's attitude; "My wife likes only Switzerland and lemonade," he said.

FAMILY, FRIENDS & OTHERS
FRIENDS FROM AIX

Throughout his life Cézanne maintained friends from his home town of Aix. The "inseparables," the childhood friends Baille, Zola, and Cézanne, kept their friendship going into adulthood. Émile Zola remained very close to Cézanne until a book published by Zola in 1886 offended Cézanne to such an extent that he ceased to communicate with the writer. The acquaintances Cézanne made at the drawing school in Aix, where he studied from 1856 to 1859, lasted many years. When Cézanne left for Paris in pursuit of Zola, who had already decided to make a home there, he found familiar faces from Aix such as Solari and Valabrègue. These young hopefuls rubbed shoulders with the exciting avant-garde in the Parisian cafés where artists and intellectuals debated the latest artistic fashions long into the night.

ACHILLE EMPERAIRE, c.1868

Emperaire was an artist from Aix who studied with Cézanne at the Académie Suisse in Paris. Cézanne was very attached to Emperaire who suffered from dwarfism. His painting portrays Emperaire's condition ruthlessly—the young man's feet are propped on a box because they would not reach the ground. However there is a sensitive handling of the face, which shows Emperaire gazing thoughtfully into the distance. Emperaire stayed with Cézanne in Paris in 1872, but only for a short time. When he left he wrote; "*I have left Cézanne—it was unavoidable, otherwise I would not have escaped the fate of the others. I found him deserted by everybody. He hasn't got a single intelligent or close friend left.*" Later in life Cézanne is reported to have wanted to destroy the picture.

Zola and Cézanne had been
intimate friends since childhood.
Zola, a highly talented writer,
became notorious for his
Realist novels such as *Nana*,
and *Germinal*, which although
causing a scandal when they were
published, today are considered to
be among the greatest French novels
of the 19th century. This painting,
found in Zola's attic after his death,
is clearly unfinished, showing Zola's
body as a few bold brushstrokes
against the cream canvas. In 1886,
Zola published a novel called
L'Oeuvre about a failed painter
named Claude Lantier. The character
was said to be based on Cézanne.
This caused a permanent break
between the two and their
friendship never recovered.

On April 4, 1886, Cézanne wrote:

> My dear Émile
>
> *I have just received* L'Oeuvre, *which you were good enough
> to send me. I thank the author of* Les Rougon-Macquart *for
> this kind token of remembrance and ask him to permit me
> to clasp his hand while thinking of bygone years. Ever
> yours under the impulse of past times.*
>
> Paul Cézanne

The letter undoubtedly refers to the relationship in the past
tense and is far more formal than his normal letters to the writer.
Some years later Zola said; "*Ah yes, Cézanne. How I regret not having
been able to push him. In my Claude Lantier I have drawn a likeness
of him that is actually too mild, for if I had wanted to tell all...!*"

JOACHIM GASQUET, 1896/7

Gasquet was a young poet from
Aix and the son of one of
Cézanne's childhood friends.
Gasquet was very taken
with Cézanne's work
and set about publishing
transcriptions of lengthy
conversations he had
with the artist. After a
time their relationship
became strained, as
was the case with
many of Cézanne's
friendships.

WHAT DO THE PAINTINGS SAY?

Sudden outbursts of wild painting characterized Cézanne's work in the 1860s and early 70s. It is difficult to understand how this fits with the rest of his work but when Cézanne's friend Zola wrote the controversial book *L'Oeuvre*, which was thought to be based on Cézanne, he said of Claude Lantier (the main character of the novel): *"It was a chaste man's passion for the flesh of women, a mad love of nudity desired and never possessed...Those girls whom he chased out of his studio he adored in his paintings; he caressed or attacked them, in tears of despair at not being able to make them sufficiently beautiful, sufficiently alive."*

The black maid in attendance in Manet's painting has a far more active role in Cézanne's picture, as she unveils the female figure to the man seated in the foreground.

Manet's *Olympia* includes a black cat representing promiscuity. The cat replaces the dog painted in Titian's version of Venus, which represented faithfulness. Cézanne includes a lapdog complete with red ribbon which suggests decadence.

A MODERN OLYMPIA, 1873

In 1867 Cézanne made a painting which he called *A Modern Olympia*. This painting was a homage to Manet's famous painting Olympia which was the sensation of the 1865 Salon. Apparently the subject came up in conversation some years later when Cézanne was staying with Dr Gachet in Auvers. The story states that Cézanne immediately took up his brushes and with uncharacteristic speed painted another canvas also called *A Modern Olympia*. This version of 1873 was exhibited at the first Impressionist exhibition in 1874. Criticism was heaped upon the exhibition. A female critic who wrote in the paper *L'Artiste* under the name Marc de Montifaud commented of *A Modern Olympia*; "*On Sunday the public saw fit to sneer at a fantastic figure that is revealed under an opium sky to a drug addict. This apparition of pink and nude flesh... has left even the most courageous gasping for breath. Mr Cézanne merely gives the impression of being a sort of madman who paints in delirium tremens.*"

OLYMPIA

Édouard Manet

Manet painted *Olympia* in 1863 but did not submit it for exhibition until 1865. Manet referred back to a well-known painting called *Venus of Urbino* painted by Titian in 1538. Manet's Olympia is a modern courtesan who is self-possessed and confident, unashamed of her nakedness. She looks directly at the viewer, thereby involving the spectator in the scene. This confrontation was shocking for the public, who were used to gazing on images of naked women safely portrayed as mythical goddesses.

This man is undoubtedly a self-portrait with Cézanne's own distinct features.

WHAT DO THE PAINTINGS SAY?
MONT SAINTE-VICTOIRE

The mountain of Sainte-Victoire dominates the landscape around Aix. Mont Sainte-Victoire became Cézanne's *motif*, his subject to which he continually returned, painting the landscape again and again. It is perhaps for his views of Sainte-Victoire that Cézanne is best known. In 1881, Cézanne's brother-in-law, Maxime Conil, purchased a house called Bellevue which stood to the southwest of the town of Aix. The house was situated on a hill overlooking the Arc valley with the mountain of Sainte-Victoire in the distance. Cézanne visited Bellevue on many occasions, setting up his canvas to paint the rural landscape, especially the view along the valley toward the flat-topped mountain. A viaduct in the middle distance formed a bold horizontal line running toward the foot of the mountain. Cézanne loved this countryside which he had known so well since childhood. He said that the subject was *"the conformation of my country."*

Mont Sainte-Victoire 1880

Cézanne painted Sainte-Victoire repeatedly in different conditions of light, exploring the form which appeared ever-changing under the harsh Provençal sun. However Cézanne's obsession was about making something with a strong underlying structure. He grew further and further away from the Impressionist painters whose fixation with the transient effects of light on color was for Cézanne "not permanent." In conversation Cézanne said to Joachim Gasquet; "Impressionism, what does it mean? It is the optical mixing of colors, do you understand? The colors are broken down on the canvas and reassembled by the eye. We had to go through that... but now we need to give a firmness, a framework to the evanescence of all things."

Mont Sainte-Victoire was the subject Cézanne chose to create this firmness, this permanence that he felt had eluded fellow painters such as Monet. It was more than just a mountain, itself the very essence of permanence. Sainte-Victoire was the foundation of Cézanne's beloved Provence countryside, the security of his family home, the solidity of his youthful friendships.

MONT SAINTE-VICTOIRE SEEN FROM LES LAUVES

When his last link with his parents was cut after his mother's death in 1897, Cézanne was drawn nearer to the mountain, taking a studio in the hills at Chemin des Lauves overlooking Aix. This painting made between 1904 and 1906, is a view of Sainte-Victoire from Les Lauves. The same motif Cézanne was painting almost 30 years earlier became increasingly abstract, with sky and ground merging together as Cézanne searched for the underlying framework in his painting.

Mont Sainte-Victoire 1885

Mont Sainte-Victoire 1890

MOUNTAINS IN PROVENCE, 1878/80

Cézanne described how
he tried to paint from nature.
This description is a telling insight
into the way the artist works, his
thought process as he struggles to
create a work of art. *"If I reach too high
or too low, everything is a mess. There
must not be a single loose strand, a single
gap through which the tension, the light,
the truth can escape. I have all the parts of
my canvas under control simultaneously.
If things are tending to diverge, I use my
instincts and my beliefs to bring them
back together again...I take the tones of
color I see to my right and my left, here,
there, everywhere, and I fix these
gradations, I bring them together...
They form lines, and become objects,
rocks, trees, without my thinking about
it. They acquire volume, they have an
effect. When these masses and weights
on my canvas correspond to the planes,
and spots which I see in my mind and
which we see with our eyes, then
my canvas closes its fingers."*

HOW WERE THEY MADE?
THE STRUCTURE OF THINGS

Cézanne was reaching for a way of painting
what was beneath the surface, the basic form of his
subject expressed and modeled in color. His fellow
Impressionist painters worked very quickly in order
to capture the fleeting impression of light on the
surface, where Cézanne worked slowly, laboriously,
using color to build solid shapes. He is famous for
his statement that he *"wanted to make of Impressionism
something solid and durable, like the art of the Museums."*
He sought to create images which represented the
subject as color and tone together, that is to
identify a color which could represent the tone
of an object and in this way build something solid
out of color alone, without the need for line or shade.
He expressed this method of working when he said:
*"I try to render perspective through color alone...
I proceed very slowly, for nature reveals herself to
me in a very complex form, and constant progress
must be made. One must see one's model correctly
and experience it in the right way, and furthermore,
express oneself with distinction and strength."*

PAUL CÉZANNE
SITTING IN
THE COUNTRY

This photograph, taken by
Cézanne's friend Émile
Bernard, shows Cézanne as
an old man in his beloved
Provençale countryside.

BEND IN THE ROAD, *c*.1900/6

Cézanne increasingly analyzed
his landscapes as ordered
brushstrokes and parallel color
blocks which are described today as
"constructive strokes." Through these
building blocks of color he attempted
to represent sunlight on the
landscape rather than provide
an impression of its effects.
Although he rejected the
Impressionist style, he still adopted
the use of complementary colors
famously used by the Impressionists,
such as setting muted blues against
oranges to create depth in the picture
plane. It is in canvases such as *Bend
in the Road* and the 1904 painting of
Sainte-Victoire (see page 17) that
historians have seen the beginnings
of Cubist and eventually Abstract art.

HOW WERE THEY MADE?
STILL LIFE

Cézanne said he wanted to conquer Paris with an apple—in other words to become famous for his modest still-life paintings. He applied the same methodical analysis to his still-life pictures as he did to his landscapes, which often resulted in the fruit rotting in the bowl before he could finish the painting, so eventually he used artificial fruit. The simple shapes of the fruit and bowls appealed to him; they were, after all, the basic spheres, cubes, and cylinders out of which all things can be said to be made. Another indication of the time he devoted to the paintings is the fact that sometimes contradicting shadows can be seen. Each time he returned to the subject he would paint exactly what he saw, even if the shadow had moved. He would spend weeks, sometimes months or longer on a painting, and if he was not happy with the result would abandon the picture or sometimes destroy it.

FLOWERS AND FRUITS, *c.*1880

Cézanne derived enormous pleasure from creating fruits which were painted with such delicacy of color and yet were given real volume and weight. It is almost as if the viewer can feel their roundness in the palm of the hand.

STILL LIFE WITH CURTAIN, *c.*1898/9

This still life was carefully arranged in order to present exactly the combination of shapes and juxtaposition of colors that Cézanne wanted.

VESSELS, BASKET AND FRUIT, 1888/90

The still life pictures appear at first glance to be simple representations of everyday objects, and yet these paintings are some of the most sophisticated images to have been created at the end of the 19th century. The artist's viewpoint has been very carefully selected and is in fact not one but several shifting viewpoints. The objects are seen from a number of different angles at the same time, so the jug appears to be tipping forward but the plane of the table top contradicts it. The distortions of perspective are deliberate so that important shapes and colors balance each other pictorially rather than present a true representation of the still life. This playfulness broke with the rules of art which had been established for generations and stretched back to the Renaissance. Cézanne flattens the perspective where it pleases him to do so, pursuing harmony of shape and color to create a painting which cares more for the "abstract" elements of composition than for a perfect illusion of objects on a table.

Here we can see an example of how this painting has varying shadows. This lemon has a shadow on the top, and light at the bottom.

The shadow and light are reversed here.

THE CARD PLAYERS, 1890/95

The Card Players is one of Cézanne's best-known works. Card players are a common subject for artists and many versions of such a scene existed before Cézanne set up his canvas. He made five versions of the scene in all. Just as in his still-life pictures and paintings of Sainte-Victoire, he painted the subject again and again exploring variations of the theme. In one version only two players are depicted, facing each other. In another three players sit around the table while another has three players, a standing onlooker and a boy at the shoulder of the central card player.

SOMBER COLORS

We can tell from the simple clothes that the figures clearly belong in the Provençale countryside and their serious expressions suggest they have a hard life. This dark gloomy atmosphere is emphasized by the somber colors used by the artist.

ABSTRACT QUALITIES OF THE IMAGE

The very symmetrical composition with eyes focused down on the cards gives the pictures a stillness which recalls Cézanne's still-life paintings. Cézanne's arrangement of people and prop-like objects is organized in a manner which deliberately sets out to present a combination of shapes and colors instead of telling the story of two men playing cards. The artist is more interested in the abstract qualities of the image than a representation of an event.

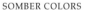

FAMOUS IMAGES

After the death of his father in 1886, Cézanne inherited a large fortune and he could have led whatever life he chose. He decided on the simple life at Jas de Bouffan, the family house in Aix, painting the surrounding countryside and whatever was close at hand. Cézanne often found models for his portrait paintings among the laborers who worked on the estate at Jas de Bouffan. He could afford to pay these workers to sit for him for long periods of time, for Cézanne was as exacting with his studies of people as he was with the still life and landscape. He painted at Jas de Bouffan, living an increasingly secluded life with his sister as well as Hortense and Paul, until he set up a new studio on the road to Les Lauves which afforded views of his favorite motif, Mont Sainte-Victoire. It appeared that Cézanne increasingly shunned contact with people, sometimes positively ducking out of sight of acquaintances he might meet in the street.

WOMAN WITH A COFFEE POT, 1890/5

It is likely that the subject for this painting was one of the servants at Jas de Bouffan, possibly the housekeeper. There is a feeling of massiveness about the form of the woman, a sense that the figure is as monumental as the mountain outside Aix that Cézanne loved to paint.

The vertical forms of the cafetière and standing spoon echo the erect pose of the woman who appears to be painted in a different plane to the table top, just as Cézanne painted conflicting perspectives in his still-life pictures.

The blues and greens of the woman's dress against the orange and burnt brown of the wall paneling and tablecloth tend to accentuate her solidity and isolate her from the background.

FAMOUS IMAGES
THE BATHERS

BATHERS, 1875/77

This is one of the earliest examples of Cézanne's
paintings of bathers in the landscape.

In 1899, the Jas de Bouffan was sold and
Cézanne moved into an apartment in Aix
with a housekeeper. His wife and son spent
most of their time in Paris, and Cézanne had
a house built at Chemin des Lauves in the
hills outside Aix. The house had a studio on
the first floor with a ceiling some five meters
high and a long narrow slit in the outer wall
in order to move large canvases. Around
1900, Cézanne returned to a favorite subject,
figures in the landscape. He had painted
a number of paintings on this theme in the
1870s and 80s, but he now concentrated
on making a number of large paintings
including the biggest canvas at over 6
and a half feet by 8 feet.

THE LARGE BATHERS, 1894-1905

This group of bathers comprises all female figures, like the other large bathers canvas. Cézanne
did not mix male and female bathers together in his pictures, possibly for fear of creating
a scene which would be considered inappropriate, and which would distract from his main
purpose of using the figures as compositional devices, completely anonymous as human beings.
However symbolic elements have been introduced into the picture and it is certain that Cézanne
would have been aware of their meaning. The dog, curled up asleep at the foot of the picture,
represents faithfulness. The fruit on the ground and
in the basket represent the loss of innocence. These
symbols have been used for centuries, and Cézanne
himself used similar references in earlier works
including *The Modern Olympia* (see page 19)
which was based on a painting by Manet.

THE LARGE BATHERS, 1906

Cézanne spent seven years working on this painting in his methodical manner, returning to the canvas on numerous occasions in order to change aspects, or to add a little, just as he did with all his paintings. The canvas, which is now in the Museum of Art in Philadelphia, was the largest Cézanne painted. It has a strong triangular-shaped center emphasized by the leaning figures and trees, and comprises a group of women—no men are present—who appear to be resting after bathing. The women are crudely depicted, and are more important for the structural shapes they present than for their individuality.

At the center of the triangle on the far side of the river are two figures and behind them a church tower. One of the figures standing on the far bank is a man with his arms folded, staring across at the women. It has been suggested that this is Cézanne himself, under the shadow of the church, looking across the river at the women, at a scene he can never reach. Several of the women are staring back toward the figure. Is this a comment on his relationship with women from whom he grew more distant as life progressed?

29

HOW WERE THEY MADE?
THE BATHERS

Cézanne would draw figures from life, although he became increasingly awkward with models, especially in unclothed poses. Instead, he started to rely upon memory and references taken from sketches and reproductions of paintings from the Old Masters in the Louvre and elsewhere, even sketches from illustrations in his sister's fashion magazines. One report mentions Cézanne using an album entitled *Le Nu au Musée du Louvre* (The Nude in the Louvre Museum), which he bought from a shop in Paris as a reference for figure studies. Wherever Cézanne did make studies from life he would use and reuse the figure in many works, treating it as a stock item which could be called upon for a number of different purposes.

A PHENOMENAL MEMORY

For his bathers series, Cézanne relied on his memory of the human form to help him create the figures. *"Painting is in here"* he said, tapping his head. Critics have found clear references in the Bathers series to known works such as Michelangelo's *Dying Slave* sculpture (above).

BATHERS

In addition to the canvases painted in oils he produced a number of pencil and watercolor sketches dominated by blues and grays. These did not serve as preparatory sketches for the oil paintings but are independent versions in their own right. Some of the watercolor and oil paintings appear unfinished because Cézanne has left areas of the paper or canvas uncovered, so the base color shows through. It is almost as if the act of filling in the canvas would have unbalanced the picture, and that the spots of white are as important as the patches of color in creating an overall harmony. This painting demonstrates the "hatching" brushstrokes that Cézanne frequently used, going in different directions to provide movement across the picture surface.

Cézanne in front of one of the *Large Bathers*

THE LARGE BATHERS—DETAIL

This detail from the sky of *The Large Bathers* (page 29) shows the way in which Cézanne applied the paint. Loose, large brushstrokes have been used to apply fairly thin coats of pigment in a very free style. The contra-angled strokes are clearly visible in this detail, and serve to animate the picture's surface when seen from a distance. The picture gives the appearance of being painted quickly, although it is known that Cézanne spent literally years working on the canvas.

31

THE AUDIENCE FOR THE PICTURES

Cézanne exhibited with the Impressionists during the 1870s and at small shows such as Les Vingt in Brussels but did not have his own exhibition until 1895, when his work was exhibited at the gallery of Paris art dealer, Ambroise Vollard. Cézanne did not need to sell his paintings to make a living as he was financially independent after the death of his father. His work was exhibited sporadically during the late 1890s, and an auction of Émile Zola's art collection on his death in 1902 saw Cézanne's paintings fetch an average of 1,500 francs. The first gallery to buy his work was the Nationalgalerie in Berlin. Shortly before his death in 1906, the art world was beginning to take notice of Cézanne's work, with 30 paintings being displayed in the 1904 Paris Salon and 10 paintings being exhibited at the Grafton Street gallery in London in 1905, thanks to the efforts of dealer Durand-Ruel. In 1907, the year after Cézanne's death, a major retrospective exhibition of his work featuring 56 paintings was held at the Paris Autumn Salon.

PORTRAIT OF VICTOR CHOCQUET, 1876/7

Victor Chocquet was a civil servant in the Ministry of Finance who was not wealthy, but nevertheless became a collector of art after befriending the Impressionist painters. Cézanne painted his portrait many times. Chocquet built up an impressive collection of paintings including 35 works by Cézanne.

DARK AND LEGENDARY

The art critic Gustave Geffroy (left) saw the exhibition organized by Ambroise Vollard and wrote the following: "*Passers-by walking into the Galerie Vollard, in rue Laffitte, will be faced with about 50 pictures: figures, landscapes, fruit, flowers, from which they can finally reach a verdict on one of the finest and greatest personalities of our time. Once that has happened, and it is high time it did happen, all that is dark and legendary about Cézanne's life will disappear, and what remains will be a rigorous and yet attractive, masterly and yet naive life's work... He will end up in the Louvre.*"

THE BATH, *c.1881*

Mary Cassatt

The American Impressionist painter Mary Cassatt met Cézanne in 1894 when they were both staying at Claude Monet's home town of Giverny. She describes her first encounter with Cézanne: *"When I first saw him, he looked like a cut-throat with large red eyeballs standing out from his head in a most ferocious manner, a rather fierce-looking pointed beard, quite grey, and an excited way of talking that positively made the dishes rattle...in spite of the total disregard for the dictionary of manners, he shows a politeness towards us which no other man here would have shown."*

PORTRAIT OF AMBROISE VOLLARD (*left detail*), 1889

A young art dealer named Ambroise Vollard who had made contact with Cézanne through his son Paul, decided to champion Cézanne's work. He arranged a one-man exhibition of Cézanne's paintings in his Paris gallery in 1895, exhibiting 50 works to a public who knew nothing of this painter from Aix.

SELF-PORTRAIT (*detail*), 1873/6

Cézanne painted the portraits of his wife, his son, friends such as Zola and Gasquet, and sometimes the servants and laborers around the family estate, but did not undertake commissions in the same way as his contemporaries, such as Renoir, did. Cézanne did not need the money from such commissions but also his very slow and methodical way of working did not lend itself to private sittings. The artist painted his own portrait repeatedly, one model he could guarantee would pose without problems, unlike his young son who could never stay still to the satisfaction of his father. This self-portrait was made around 1875. The critic Louis Vauxcelles described Cézanne in an article: *"Cézanne is a legendary figure with a coarse bristly face, a body wrapped in a haulier's rough woollen greatcoat. But this Cézanne is a master."*

A LASTING IMPRESSION

THE FATHER
OF US ALL

Cézanne was described
by Picasso (shown left
with Jaqueline Roque)
as *"My one and only
master... Cézanne was like
the father of us all."*

Cézanne's art is considered today to be of profound importance to the development of Western art in the 20th century. Historians point to Cézanne's search for the underlying structure in his compositions as the foundation of modern art, from which Cubism and then Abstraction came. He has never been considered an Impressionist painter despite being one of that small group who first exhibited a new way of painting which was so shocking to its public. It is above all Cézanne's obsession with formal elements of composition and his use of color as tone, rather than the Impressionist pursuit of light on surface, that makes his art so important to those who followed. Cézanne's work made it possible for artists to start to question what they saw, the way in which they saw it, and how they interpreted and represented what was in front of them.

HOMAGE TO CÉZANNE

Maurice Denis

Many artists of different persuasion found something to admire in Cézanne. The Cubists such as Braque and also Picasso considered him the father of Cubism. Symbolist painters such as Gauguin and Maurice Denis looked to Cézanne's work as a source of inspiration even though Cézanne himself thought the Symbolist work too concerned with surface decoration. In 1900, Maurice Denis painted a homage to Cézanne. This painting shows a group of artists gathered round the Cézanne painting *Still Life with Compotier* which had once been owned by Paul Gauguin. Included in the picture are Maurice Denis and his wife, Odilon Redon, Pierre Bonnard, Édouard Vuillard, Paul Serusier, and the art dealer Ambroise Vollard.

L'ESTAQUE

Georges Braque

In a letter to the artist Émile Bernard, Cézanne wrote: *"Treat nature by means of the cylinder, the sphere, the cone, with everything in its proper perspective so that each side of an object or plane is directed towards a central point. Lines parallel to the horizon give breadth, that is a section of nature... Lines perpendicular to this horizon give depth. But nature for us men is more depth than surface..."* This letter has become very famous because when Cézanne referred to seeing nature in terms of the basic shapes, it appeared that he was already looking at things in the Cubist's way. Cubist art first came to the public's attention in 1907 when Braque exhibited a painting at the Paris Salon and Matisse commented that he had reduced everything to little cubes. Cubism has been seen by art historians as the breaking point between representational art and abstract art that was to dominate the 20th century.

MONT SAINTE-VICTOIRE, 1905/6

A few weeks before he died Cézanne wrote to his son in Paris: *"I must tell you that as a painter I am becoming more clear-sighted before Nature, but with me the realization of my senses is always painful. I cannot attain the intensity that is unfolded before my senses. I do not have the magnificent richness of coloring that animates Nature."*

LES LAUVES

The studio that Cézanne had built at Les Lauves remains today as a small museum to the artist. Unfortunately it was not possible to preserve the view across to Sainte-Victoire which was so important to Cézanne—it is now obscured by apartment blocks.

DID YOU KNOW?
FASCINATING FACTS ABOUT THE ARTIST AND THE TIMES IN WHICH HE WORKED

• Cézanne made friends with Émile Zola at school by defending the younger boy against bullies.

• As an adult, Cézanne returned to places that he and his friends Zola and Baille had explored when they were schoolboys. Many of the locations appear in his paintings.

• Despite his wealth, as he had been a hat maker, Cézanne's father was never accepted by middle class society, so he hoped that his son would earn respect as a lawyer. Unfortunately for Monsieur Cézanne, Paul had other ideas—and disliked fashionable society anyway.

• Cézanne married Hortense seventeen years after they first met, when their son Paul was fourteen years old.

• As a young man, Cézanne had a pet dog called Black who rarely left his side. He included him in several paintings. (He is in the painting *Apotheosis of Delacroix* on pages 8–9).

• In 1874, after Cézanne had participated in the first Impressionist exhibition, his former art tutor asked to see what he had exhibited. When Cézanne showed him the paintings, the tutor looked horrified and walked away without another word.

• Gauguin admired Cézanne enormously and bought five of his paintings from a dealer in Paris. He wrote to their mutual friend Pissarro, asking to be told if Cézanne revealed anything about his painting method. It was a flattering query showing how highly Gauguin esteemed Cézanne, but when Pissarro told him, Cézanne became angry and accused Gauguin of trying to steal his ideas.

• Although Cézanne never spoke to Zola again after the publication of *L'Oeuvre* or *The Masterpiece* which ridiculed Cézanne, when Zola died in an accident in September 1902, Cézanne shut himself in his studio and wept.

- The Impressionist Gustave Caillebotte was wealthy and he supported his friends by buying their works when they were poor. After his unexpected death at the age of forty-six, Parisian art officials learned that he had bequeathed his collection of paintings to the Louvre, instructing that they should be displayed together there. The art officials did not want them!

  Eventually, they were made to select some works, but would not accept twenty-seven out of the sixty-seven paintings, which included works by Cézanne. Most of the rejected works of the legacy were bought by an American inventor and art collector, Dr Albert C. Barnes, who began the Barnes Foundation in Pennsylvania.

- The Salon rejected every painting that Cézanne submitted until 1882, when a work he had painted sixteen years earlier was accepted—but only because his friend Antoine Guillemet was on the selection committee and pretended that he had taught Cézanne.

- Cézanne was rather sensitive about his unpopularity and one day at a party at Monet's house, Monet tried to make him feel more accepted by announcing how pleased everyone was to see him. Cézanne thought they were mocking him and ran away.

- In 1899, Maxime Conil, who was married to Cézanne's youngest sister Rose, wanted to sell the Jas de Bouffan, the Cézanne family house, because he needed his wife's share of the money. Cézanne had spent most of his life there, but reluctantly agreed.

- Over his career, Cézanne painted more than 200 still lifes.

- In many of his still life paintings, he used the same props, never tiring of exploring similar shapes, colors, and textures.

- Throughout their lives, Cézanne and Hortense rarely lived with each other. Even after they were married, Cézanne spent most of his time at the Jas de Bouffan with his mother and unmarried sister Marie, while Hortense lived elsewhere with their son.

- Cézanne's friends and family did not like Hortense. His friends nicknamed her "The Ball" because of the shape of her head.

- Cézanne painted the Mont Sainte-Victoire over sixty times. Fascinated by the craggy and uneven shapes, he painted it from many different angles, using bold blocks and patches of color.

- Cézanne worked tirelessly throughout his life, always trying to achieve his inner vision. Because he was so dedicated, he even worked through a storm when he was 67 years old—and he died from pneumonia eight days later.

- In 2000, a painting by Cézanne was stolen from a museum in Oxford, UK.

SUMMARY TIMELINE OF
THE ARTIST & HIS CONTEMPORARIES

THE LIFE OF CÉZANNE

~1839~
Photography is invented in the year of Cézanne's birth

~1839~
Émile Zola, Claude Monet, and Auguste Rodin are born in Paris; the Romantic landscape painter Caspar David Friedrich dies

~1841~
The Impressionist painters Berthe Morisot, Auguste Renoir, and Frédéric Bazille are born

~1843~
Charles Dickens' *A Christmas Carol* is first published; J. M. W. Turner paints *Light and Colour (Goethe's theory)*

~1848~
Paul Gauguin is born; in England the Pre-Raphaelite Brotherhood is founded by William Holman Hunt, John Everett Millais and Dante

Gabriel Rossetti; the California Gold Rush begins and revolutions erupt all over Europe as many people are out of work and hungry

~1851~
The first World Exhibition is held in the UK in London's Hyde Park with over 13,000 exhibits; Holman Hunt paints *The Hireling Shepherd*

~1852~
In the year that Cézanne begins at the Collège Bourbon, the French President Louis Bonaparte is crowned Emperor Napoleon III

~1853~
An outbreak of yellow fever kills 7,790 people in New Orleans; Vincent van Gogh is born

~1857~
The first world economic crisis begins in New York; Jean-François Millet paints *The Gleaners*

~1858~
Zola moves to Paris; after a second try, Cézanne passes his school final exams with an average mark and enrols in a law course in Aix-en-Provence

~1859~
In the year that his father buys the Jas de Bouffan, Cézanne wins second prize at the Municipal Drawing School in Aix

~1861~
Abraham Lincoln becomes President of the United States; the American Civil War begins

~1862~
Jean-Auguste-Dominic Ingres paints *The Turkish Bath*; Otto von Bismarck becomes Prime Minister of Prussia; Gustav Klimt is born

~1863~
Cézanne exhibits at the Salon des Refusés where Manet also exhibits his infamous *Le Déjeuner sur l'Herbe*

~1865~
The end of the American Civil War and the abolition of slavery; Cézanne's paintings are once again rejected by the Salon

~1866~
The Russian artist Wassily Kandinsky is born; Cézanne produces a portrait of his father reading the newspaper *L'Évenement*; in response to Manet's earlier work, Monet completes his huge painting, *Le Déjeuner sur l'Herbe*

~1869~
Henri Matisse is born; in the year he meets Hortense at the Académie Suisse in Paris, Cézanne paints *Paul Alexis Reading to Émile Zola*

~1870~
The French fight the Germans during the Franco-Prussian War and Cézanne avoids the army by hiding in L'Estaque

~1872~
Cézanne completes his painting *The Apotheosis of Delacroix*; the artists Mondrian and Beardsley are born

~1873~
Cézanne spends time in Pontoise and Auvers-sur-Oise where he paints *The House of the Hanged Man* and *Dr Gachet's House* and meets Julian 'Père' Tanguy who accepts many of his paintings in exchange for art materials

~1874~
After the first independent exhibition, the term Impressionism is invented

~1875~
Cézanne meets Victor Chocquet who buys several of his paintings, Père Tanguy starts exhibiting and selling works by Cézanne at 50 francs each; the painters Millet and Corot die

~1877~
The beginning of color photography; the death of Courbet; Cézanne participates in the third Impressionist exhibition

~1882~
The year after Picasso is born in Spain, Georges Braque is born in France; Cézanne is accepted for the Salon for the first time; the painter Edward Hopper is born

~1883~
Manet dies; Monet and Renoir visit Cézanne in Aix-en-Provence on their return from a tour of the Mediterranean coast

~1890~
In the year that he paints *Wheatfield with Crows*, Van Gogh shoots himself and dies two days later; three of

Cézanne's paintings are exhibited in Brussels

~1895~
Cézanne paints the Bibémus Quarry and the Mont Sainte-Victoire; Frederick Leighton paints *Flaming June*

~1896~
The first Olympic Games of modern times is held in Athens; an earthquake and tsunami in Sanriku, Japan kills 27,000; the first x-ray photograph is taken; Frederick Leighton dies

~1901~
Cézanne buys land on the 'Chemin des Lauves' where he creates his studio; Queen Victoria dies after reigning for sixty-four years; Toulouse-Lautrec dies

~1904~
Cézanne's paintings are displayed in an entire room at the Salon d'Automne, at the same exhibition, paintings by Matisse and other artists are labeled *Les Fauves*, meaning *Wild Beasts*; the painters Arshile Gorky and Willem de Kooning are born

~1906~
In the year of Cézanne's death, Georges Braque paints *L'Estaque* and Picasso paints *Les Demoiselles d'Avignon*

WHAT DID HE SAY?

Here are a few of the many things Cézanne said about art:

• "Art is a harmony parallel with nature"

• "Doubtless there are things in nature which have not yet been seen. If an artist discovers them, he opens the way for his successors"

• "I could paint for … a thousand years without stopping and I would still feel as though I knew nothing"

• "The contrasts and relations of tones—there you have the secret of drawing and modeling"

• "My age and health will never allow me to realize the dream of art I've been pursuing all my life"

• "Treat nature by the cylinder, the sphere, the cone"

• "Drawing and color are not distinct, everything in nature is colored"

• "The artist makes things concrete and gives them individuality"

• "The day is coming when a single carrot, freshly observed, will set off a revolution"

• "I want to make Impressionism something solid and lasting, like the art in museums"

• "The world doesn't understand me and I don't understand the world, that's why I've withdrawn from it"

• "There are two things in the painter, the eye and the mind; each of them should aid the other"

• "With an apple I will astonish Paris"

• "Perhaps I was born too early"

• "An art which isn't based on feeling isn't an art at all"

• "Painting from nature is not copying the object, it is realizing one's sensations"

A WORK IN CLOSE-UP

From the time he met her, Cézanne painted Hortense more than any other model. In painting her, he treated her as one of his still lifes – measuring spaces, checking forms and shapes, and working out every color and tone before making a mark on the canvas. He took so long that most people grew bored sitting for him, but Hortense was patient, so he painted nearly thirty portraits of her.

Painting this just before the third Impressionist exhibition and nine years before he married Hortense, Cézanne took meticulous care in applying small patches, or "taches" of different colors, creating a tapestry-like effect.

Hortense's face is painted in patches too and does not look realistic as it was not meant to. Cézanne was not interested in capturing her personality, but in showing solidity and structure.

The stripes on the skirt are built up with Cézanne's "taches" of color, mainly greens and blues mixed with white.

Some brush marks seem sketchy, but every one was placed with care.

Even Hortense's hands are created with small marks of broken color, rather than fine details.

Rarely satisfied with his paintings, Cézanne hardly ever signed them.

Cézanne left nothing to chance, everything was planned, so here curved and geometric shapes and warm and cool colors contrast with each other across the work.

Madame Cézanne in a Red Armchair, c.1877,
oil on canvas, 28 x 22in/72.4 x 55.9cm,
Museum of Fine Arts, Boston, Massachusetts, USA

WHERE TO SEE THIS ARTIST'S WORKS IN THE USA

There are plenty of places to see Cézanne's work across the USA. Not all works are permanently on display though, so it is a good idea to check before visiting.

The Art Institute
of Chicago,
Chicago, Illinois
(www.artic.edu)

The Detroit Institute
of Arts,
Detroit, Michigan
(www.dia.org)

Fine Arts Museums
of San Francisco,
San Francisco, California
(www.famsf.org)

The Guggenheim Museum,
New York
(www.guggenheim.org)

J. Paul Getty Museum,
Los Angeles, California
(www.getty.edu)

The Metropolitan
Museum,
New York
(www.metmuseum.org)

Museum of Fine Arts,
Houston, Texas
(www.mfah.org)

Norton Simon Museum,
Pasadena, California
(www.nortonsimon.org)

Museum of Fine Arts,
Boston, Massachusetts
(www.mfa.org)

Museum of Modern Art,
New York
(www.moma.org)

The National Gallery
of Art,
Washington D.C.
(www.nga.gov)

Nelson-Atkins Museum
of Art,
Kansas City, Missouri
(www.nelson-atkins.org)

Carnegie Museum of Art,
Pittsburgh, Pennsylvania
(www.cmoa.org)

Hammer Museum,
Los Angeles, California
(hammer.ucla.edu)

Indianapolis Museum
of Art,
Indianapolis, Indiana
(www.imamuseum.org)

Addison Gallery of
American Art,
Andover, Massachusetts
(accessaddison.andover.edu)

Kimbell Art Museum,
Fort Worth, Texas
(www.kimbellart.org)

Memorial Art Gallery
of the University
of Rochester,
New York
(magart.rochester.edu)

Minneapolis Institute
of Art,
Minneapolis, Minnesota
(www.artsmia.org)

St. Louis Art Museum,
St. Louis, Missouri
(stlouis.art.museum)

Smith College Museum
of Art,
Northampton,
Massachusetts
(www.smith.edu)

The Barnes Foundation,
Philadelphia, Pennsylvania
(www.barnesfoundation.org)

Worcester Art Museum,
Worcester, Massachusetts
(www.worcesterart.org)

Yale University Art Gallery,
New Haven, Connecticut
(artgallery.yale.edu)

WHERE TO SEE THIS ARTIST'S
WORKS IN THE REST OF THE WORLD

The State
Hermitage Museum,
St. Petersburg, Russia
(www.hermitage
museum.org)

The Fitzwilliam Museum,
Cambridge, England
(www.fitzmuseum.
cam.ac.uk)

Louvre Museum, Paris,
France
(www.louvre.fr)

Musée d'Orsay,
Paris, France
(www.musee-orsay.fr)

National Galleries
of Scotland,
Edinburgh, Scotland
(www.nationalgalleries.org)

Neue Pinakothek,
Munich, Germany
(www.pinakothek.de)

Art Gallery of Ontario,
Toronto, Canada
(www.ago.net)

Ashmolean Museum,
Oxford, England
(www.ashmolean.org)
Bilbao Fine Arts Museum,
Bilbao, Spain
(www.museobilbao.com)

The Courtauld Institute
of Arts,
London, England
(www.courtauld.ac.uk)

E. G. Bürhle Collection,
Zürich, Switzerland
(www.buehrle.ch)

Finnish National Gallery
Art Collections,
Helsinki, Finland
(kokoelmat.fng.fi)

Kunstmuseum Basel,
Basel, Switzerland
(www.kunstmuseumbasel.ch)

Musée de l'Orangerie,
Paris, France
(www.musee-orangerie.fr)

Museum of Geneva,
Geneva, Switzerland
(www.ville-ge.ch)

National Gallery
of Victoria,
Victoria, Australia
(www.ngv.vic.gov.au)

National Museum
of Western Art,
Tokyo, Japan
(www.tnm.go.jp)

National Museum
and Gallery of Wales,
Cardiff, Wales
(www.museumwales.ac.uk)

Walker Art Gallery
Liverpool, England
(www.liverpoolmuseums.
org.uk)

New Carlsberg Glyptotek,
Copenhagen, Denmark
(www.glyptoteket.dk)

National Gallery,
London, England
(www.nationalgallery.
org.uk)

Oskar Reinhart
Collection,
Winterthur, Switzerland
(www.roemerholz.ch)

Österreichische Galerie
Belvedere,
Vienna, Austria
(www.belvedere.at)

Pushkin State Museum
of Fine Arts,
Moscow, Russia
(www.museum.ru)

Staatsgalerie,
Stuttgart, Germany
(www.staat
sgalerie.de)

Tate Gallery,
London, England
(www.tate.org.uk)

The Ordrupgaard
Collection,
Charlottenlund, Denmark
(www.ordrupgaard.dk)

Museo Thyssen-
Bornemisza,
Madrid, Spain
(www.museothyssen.org)

Von der Heydt-Museum,
Wuppertal, Germany
(www.von-der-heydt-
museum.de)

FURTHER READING & WEBSITES

BOOKS

Paul Cézanne
(Artists in their World)
Nathaniel Harris, Franklin
Watts, 2006

Paul Cézanne:
How He Amazed the
World (Adventures in Art)
Angela Wenzel,
Prestel, 2005

Paul Cézanne:
A Painter's Journey,
Robert Burleigh,
Harry N. Abrams, Inc, 2006

Paul Cézanne
(Art Profiles for Kids),
Kathleen Tracy,
Mitchell Lane Publishers,
2007

Paul Cézanne
(Meet the Artist),
Melody S. Mis,
Powerkids Press, 2007

Color your own
Cézanne Paintings,
Dover Publications Inc, 2009

Paul Cézanne
(The Life and Work of),
Sean Connolly,
Heinemann Library, 2007

Cézanne (World's
Greatest Artists Series),
Edmund Swinglehurst,
Siena, 1995

Paul Cézanne
(Getting to know the
World's Greatest Artists),
Mike Venezia,
Franklin Watts, 1998

Monet and Impressionists
for Kids,
Carol Sabbeth,
Cappella Books, 2002

Favorite Classic Artists,
Liz Gogerly,
Wayland, 2007

Discovering Great Artists,
*MaryAnn F. Kohl
and Kim Solga*,
Brilliant Publications, 2003

Art Activity Book:
Cézanne,
Mila Boutan,
Chronicle Books, 1996

Impressionism
(Eyewitness Books),
Jude Welton,
Dorling Kindersley, 2000

WEBSITES

www.ibiblio.org/wm/paint/
auth/cézanne/

www.theartgallery.com.au/
kidsart/learn/cézanne/

www.atelier-
cézanne.com/aix-en-
provence.html

www.nga.gov/exhibitions/
cézanneinfo.shtm

www.artchive.com/theory/
schapiro/frame1.html

www.nationalgallery.org.uk
/artists/paul-cézanne

www.constable.net/
arthistory/glo-
cézanne.html

GLOSSARY

Apotheosis—admiration, highest respect

Avant-garde—a person or group who is at the forefront of new ideas and techniques, especially in the arts

Bequeathed—handing down something in a will

Expressionism—this art movement moved away from the naturalism of movements like Impressionism to express strong emotions through exaggerated line, simplified forms, and color

Hatching—drawing parallel lines to build tone in a drawing or painting. Cross-hatching is shading with two sets of parallel lines, one crossing the other. It is often used to depict dark tones rather than filling an area with solid color

Infamous—having a bad reputation

Motif—a distinctive idea or theme which is often repeated by an artist and applies to many kinds of art forms such as music, painting, and literature. One of Cézanne's main motifs was Mont Sainte-Victoire, which he painted repeatedly during his lifetime

Oeuvre—a French term which is used to describe the entire output of one artist. An Oeuvre catalogue, therefore, attempts to give a record of every work produced by the artist. The term can also apply to musicians and writers. Zola's book, which caused a rift with Cézanne was called *L'Oeuvre*, and was a play on words

Sandro Botticelli—an influential painter who lived and worked in Florence at the end of the 15th century. His best-known works, such as *The Birth of Venus*, use pagan and Christian imagery together and are painted in the style that became known as the early Renaissance

Still life—a painting of a collection of natural or manmade objects that do not move such as fruit, jugs, bowls, flowers, and so on. Some artists choose to paint objects that symbolize other things, while some artists simply enjoy painting the objects for themselves

Taches—small patches of paint

INDEX

ACKNOWLEDGMENTS

Picture Credits t=top, b=bottom, c=center, l=left, r=right, OFC=outside front cover.

AKG; 7r, 14r, 34tl. Bridgeman Art Library (London); 6tl, 12/13t, 26t & 26cr & 26bl, 30l, 32tl, 32bl, 32/33t, 34/35t. Giraudon; 6/7c, 8tl, 8/9b, 9t & 9br, 10tl, 10/11b, 10/11t, 12/13b, 14tl, 15r, 16cb, 16/17t, 17bl & 17br, 18bl & 18cl & 18/19t & 19br, 20bl, 20/21b, 21br, 21tr, 22tl, 23, 24tl, 24/25b & 25br, 25t, 27bl & 27c & 27br, 28tl, 28bl & 28/29b & 30br & 31bl, 29t & 29br, 32/33c, 33br, 34bl, 34/35c, 35br. Musée de la Ville de Paris, Musée du Petit-Palais/Giraudon/The Bridgeman Art Library; OFCb. Musée d'Orsay, Paris/Giraudon/The Bridgeman Art Library; OFC (main image), OFCt. Réunion des Musées Nationaux © RMN/R.G.Ojeda; 22cb, 31cr. Roger-Viollet © Harlingue-Viollet; 6cb. Roger-Viollet © Collection Viollet; 11br & 36ct. Staatsgalerie Moderner Kunst, Munich/Giraudon/The Bridgeman Art Library; OFCc. Tate Gallery (London); 13br.

NOTE TO READERS
The website addresses are correct at the time of publishing. However, due to the ever-changing nature of the Internet, websites and content may change. Some websites can contain links that are unsuitable for children. The publisher is not responsible for changes in content or website addresses. We advise that Internet searches should be supervised by an adult.

The 21st-Century Voter